I0201637

Air Pollution

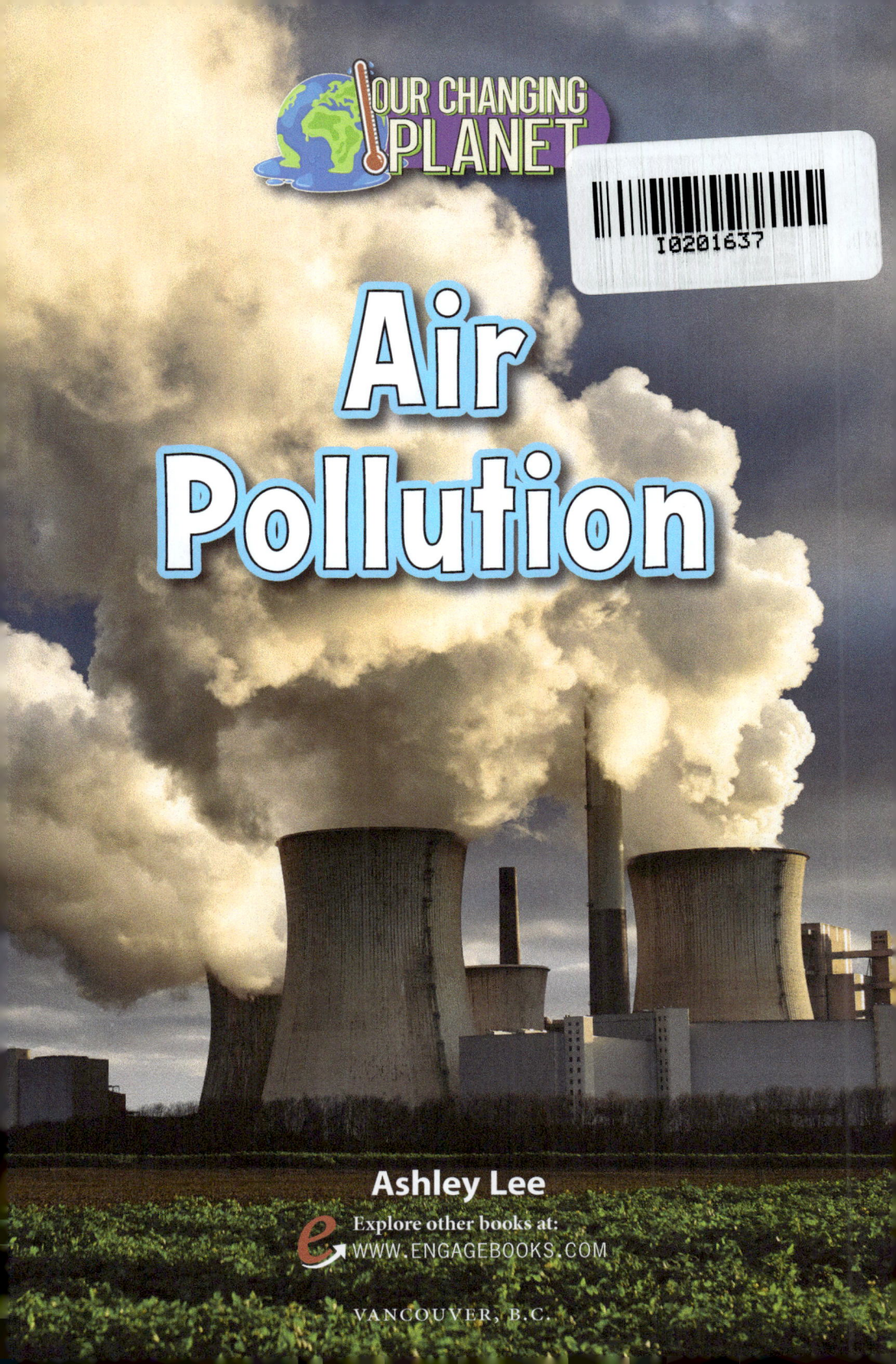

Ashley Lee

Explore other books at:
WWW.ENGAGEBOOKS.COM

VANCOUVER, B.C.

WWW.ENGAGEBOOKS.COM

Air Pollution - Our Changing Planet: *Level 3*
Lee, Ashley 1995 –
Text © 2023 Engage Books
Design © 2023 Engage Books

Edited by: A.R. Roumanis and Melody Sun
Design by: Mandy Christiansen

Text set in Montserrat Regular.
Chapter headings set in Animated Gothic Light.

FIRST EDITION / FIRST PRINTING

LIBRARY AND ARCHIVES CANADA CATALOGUING IN PUBLICATION

Title: Air pollution / Ashley Lee.
Names: Lee, Ashley, 1995- author.
Description: Series statement: Our changing planet

Identifiers: Canadiana (print) 20230505473 | Canadiana (ebook) 20230505481
ISBN 97-8-177476-887-7 (hardcover)
ISBN 978-1-77476-888-4 (softcover)
ISBN 978-1-77476-889-1 (epub)
ISBN 978-1-77476-890-7 (pdf)

Subjects:
LCSH: Air—Pollution—Juvenile literature.
LCSH: Air—Pollution—Prevention—Juvenile literature.
LCSH: Nature—Effect of human beings on—Juvenile literature.

Classification: LCC TD883.13 .L44 2023 | DDC J363.739/2—DC23

This project has been made possible in part
by the Government of Canada.

Canadä

Contents

What Is Air Pollution?

Air pollution is when the air gets dirty. Chemicals, gas, and small drops of **liquid** all make the air dirty. Something that pollutes the air is called a pollutant.

Air pollution can happen inside buildings like homes or schools. This is called indoor air pollution. Outdoor air pollution is when the air outside is polluted.

KEY WORD

Liquid: something like water that flows freely and is not solid.

Indoor air pollution is often worse than outdoor air pollution because the dirty air gets trapped by walls.

A Closer Look

Air pollution is common in big cities. Sometimes tall buildings or mountains will stop pollution from moving away from a city. This air pollution turns into a cloud called smog.

The word "smog" comes from combining the words "smoke" and "fog."

Wind spreads air pollution all around the world. It can carry dirty air thousands of miles away from where it came from. It can even carry pollutants across countries and oceans.

Causes of Air Pollution 1

Sometimes air pollution is caused by natural things. Volcanoes and forest fires can put smoke and ash into the air. Strong winds can cause dust storms that carry dirt through the air.

Air pollution can also come from the ocean. Large waves can spray harmful things like **bacteria** into the air. This pollution is then spread by strong winds.

KEY WORD

Bacteria: tiny living things that can sometimes cause illness.

Causes of Air Pollution 2

Most air pollution comes from human activities. Harmful chemicals are created and put into the air when garbage in landfills breaks down. **Aerosol cans** and cigarettes also put harmful chemicals into the air.

KEY WORD

Aerosol cans: containers that spray things like paint when you press a button on top.

Fossil fuels are things like coal, oil, and gas that people use to make energy. When people burn these fuels to make electricity for houses, cars, or **factories**, they create smoke and gases that go into the air. This is one of the main causes of air pollution.

Air Pollution and Climate Change

Climate change is a change in the average temperature over a long period of time. Earth is getting warmer because of climate change. Warmer temperatures can cause bad weather events or make plants and animals sick.

Air pollution is making climate change worse. Gas from burning fossil fuels traps heat around Earth. This causes Earth to warm up.

Gases that trap heat around Earth are called greenhouse gases.

Effects on the Planet

Acid rain is rain that becomes polluted and harmful. It happens when gases from factories and cars mix with the clouds and fall down as rain. This polluted rain can damage trees, harm animals, and make lakes and rivers unhealthy for fish and other creatures.

Air pollution can also affect how plants grow. It can make fewer plants grow and can also make plants grow smaller. Air pollution can also make plants weaker and make it easier for them to get diseases.

Effects on Humans

Air pollution can make someone's eyes, nose, and throat itchy or uncomfortable. It can even make it hard for people to breathe. Because of this, some people cannot run and play outside if air pollution is really bad.

Breathing in dirty air can also make people sick. When people breathe in dirty air for a long time, they may get diseases in their heart or lungs. About 6.7 million people die every year because of air pollution.

Children and older people are more likely to get sick from air pollution.

Air Pollution Around the World 1

The Bodélé Depression in Chad used to be a lake. The lake had lots of sand at the bottom. This sand is now one of the largest sources of dust pollution in the world. Strong winds in the area sometimes carry the dust across the ocean to the United States.

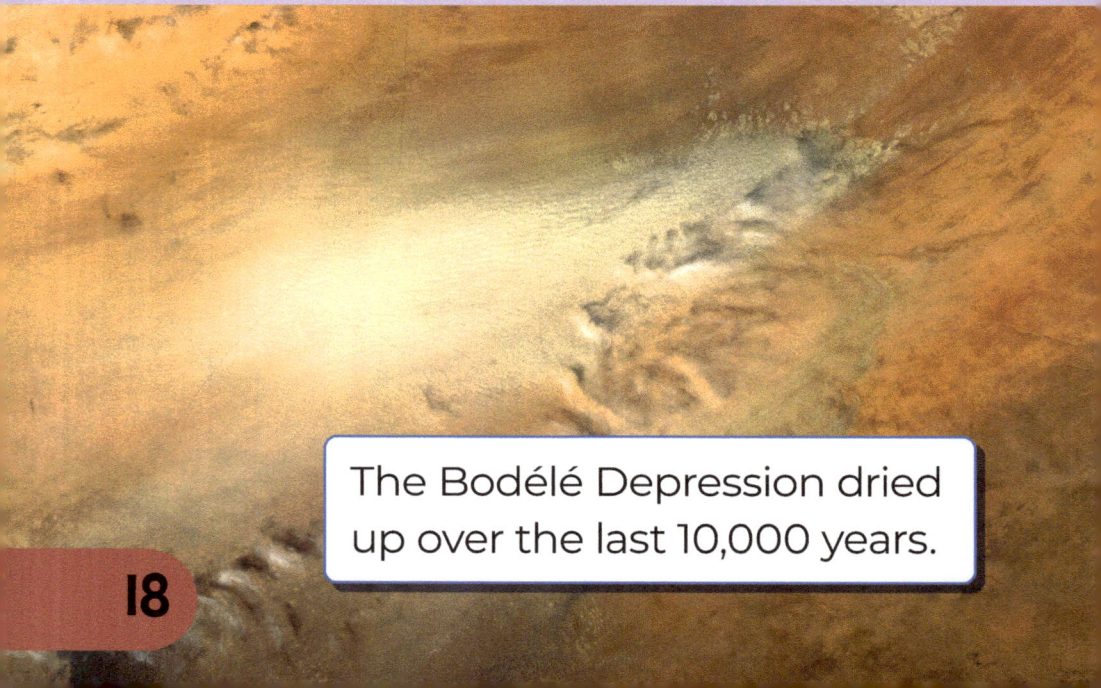

The Bodélé Depression dried up over the last 10,000 years.

China burns a lot of fossil fuels. They put more **carbon dioxide** into the air than any other country. In Beijing in 2013, the smog was so bad that airplanes could not fly and roads had to be closed.

Carbon dioxide: a greenhouse gas created by burning fossil fuels.

Air Pollution Around the World 2

Norilsk, Russia, is known for **mining** metals. When they take this metal out and melt it down, it puts a chemical called sulfur dioxide into the air. The city releases so much sulfur dioxide that it can be seen by satellites in space.

KEY WORD

Mining: digging things out from deep within the ground.

In June 2023, smoke from wildfires in Canada was carried by wind to the United States. The air pollution in New York State was some of the worst the state has ever seen in known history. The sky was orange, school activities were canceled, and people had to stay inside.

Air Pollution Solutions 1

Lots of countries and businesses are trying to burn fewer fossil fuels. They are using renewable energy sources instead. Renewable energy comes from things like wind and sunlight that cannot be used up.

Some countries are even charging companies for the greenhouse gases they put into the air. This is called a carbon tax. It encourages companies to use renewable energy instead.

Air Pollution Solutions 2

Many people are buying electric cars. Electric cars do not burn gas to run, so they do not put greenhouse gases into the air. They have a battery that gets charged with electricity instead.

Some cities are creating bike lanes on roads. These are areas of the road where cars cannot go. This allows people to get around using bikes instead of cars.

The Helpers

The Clean Air Fund works with other groups to collect information about air pollution. They use this information to help governments make rules about keeping the air clean. They also raise money to give to other groups and projects that are helping to stop air pollution.

Moms Clean Air Force is a group of parents who are fighting for cleaner air for their children. They help teach others about the effects of air pollution. They also support governments who are trying to make changes to make the air cleaner.

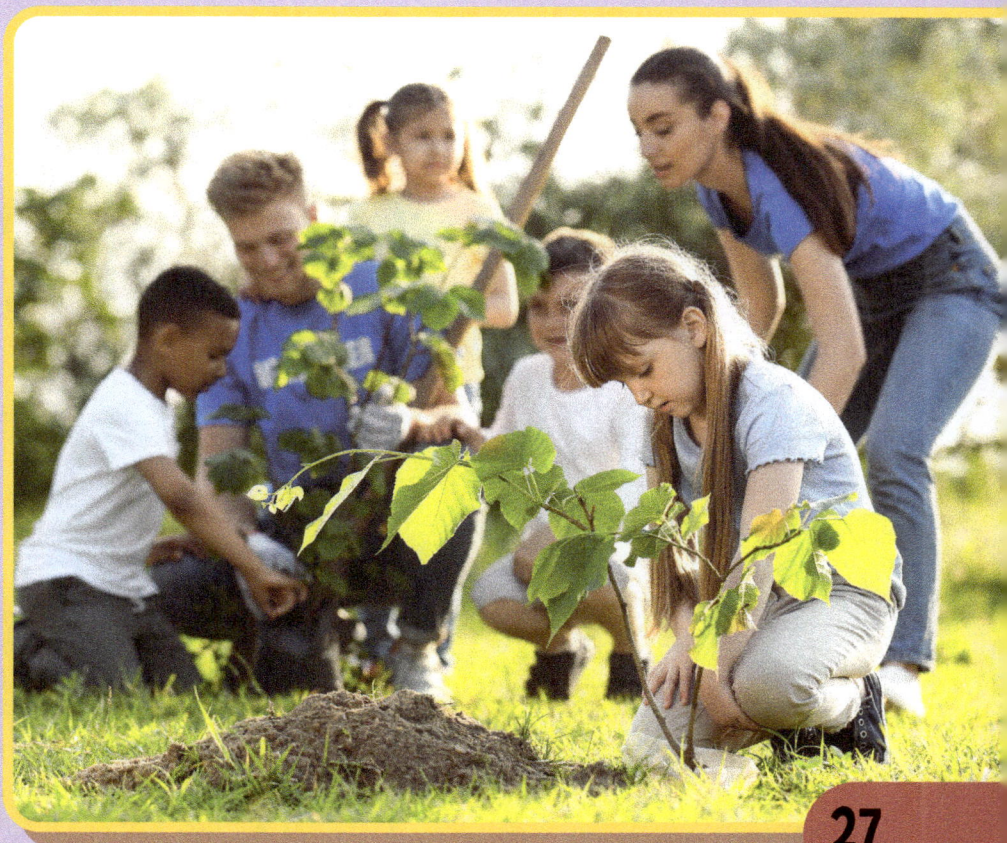

How Can You Help?

Recycle instead of throwing things in the trash. By reusing materials that have been recycled to make new things, factories do not have to make as much. Recycling also helps keep waste out of landfills.

Plant trees and plants. They help clean the air by soaking up carbon dioxide. They also release clean oxygen into the air. Humans and animals need clean oxygen to breathe.

Quiz

Test your knowledge of air pollution by answering the following questions. The questions are based on what you have read in this book. The answers are listed on the bottom of the next page.

1 What makes the air dirty?

2 Where is air pollution common?

3 Where does most air pollution come from?

4 What are gases that trap heat called?

5 Who is more likely to get sick from air pollution?

6 What should you do instead of throwing things in the trash?

Explore Other Level 3 Readers.

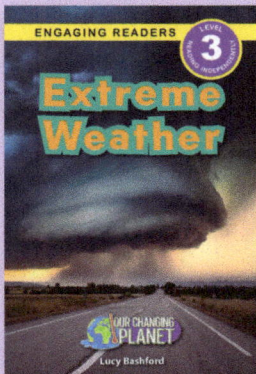

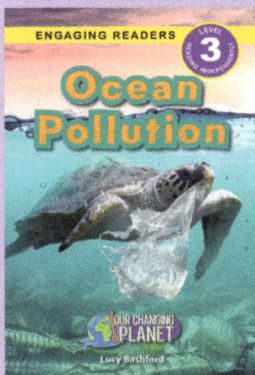

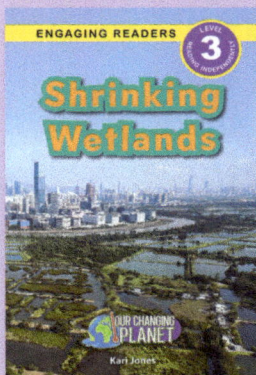

ENGAGING READERS — LEVEL 3
Climate Change
OUR CHANGING PLANET
Sarah Harvey

ENGAGING READERS — LEVEL 3
Extreme Weather
OUR CHANGING PLANET
Lucy Bashford

ENGAGING READERS — LEVEL 3
Habitat Loss
OUR CHANGING PLANET
Lucy Bashford

ENGAGING READERS — LEVEL 3
Ocean Pollution
OUR CHANGING PLANET
Lucy Bashford

ENGAGING READERS — LEVEL 3
Shrinking Wetlands
OUR CHANGING PLANET
Kari Jones

ENGAGING READERS — LEVEL 3
Diabetes
Mind and Body
Kit Caudron-Robinson

ENGAGING READERS — LEVEL 3
Obesity
Mind and Body
Kit Caudron-Robinson

ENGAGING READERS — LEVEL 3
Autism
Mind and Body
AJ Knight

ENGAGING READERS — LEVEL 3
Vision Loss
Mind and Body
Hannalora Leavitt & Sarah Harvey

Visit www.engagebooks.com/readers

Answers: 1. Chemicals, gas, and small drops of liquid 2. In big cities 3. Human activities 4. Greenhouse gases 5. Children and older people 6. Recycle

www.ingramcontent.com/pod-product-compliance
Lightning Source LLC
Chambersburg PA
CBHW051234020426
42331CB00016B/3363